RESILIENT BEING

THE POWER OF A STRONG WILL

SENORITA JOYCE

To my Mom, Mrs. Joyce Lobo

who has always been supportive,

not only of this book but my whole life,

Love you Mom, To the moon and back.

Contents

Acknowledgements

vii

I blame all of you, collating this book has been such an agony. A casual reader may perhaps, exempt themselves from excessive guilt. But for those of you who have supported me throughout and have been my strenght (Oscar, Oliver, Oreo, Sunny, Rocky and Dad) I owe this to you guys.

About The Author

''Senorita Joyce'' (born 10 Sep 1991) is an Indian Author & Social Activist. Working with various NGOs her work focuses on Women Empowerment, Child Rights & Education.

Senorita Joyce was born and brought up in the City of Dreams "Aamchi Mumbai". In a traditional Catholic household. Her father Stanley Lobo belongs to the service industry and Mother Joyce Lobo was an entrepreneur. She did her schooling from St. Charle's High School (Vakola) and went on to pursue her Junior College from St, Marys (Kalina). Later Graduating with a dual degree (B,A - Economics and BCA) from IME, Delhi. An IIM - Rohtak Allumni . She started her career as an Event Coordinator, but left it only to pursue her Dream Job into the recruitment industry. Penned her first article "Friendship is a priceless gift" in the 6th standard which happened to feature in the "Teenager Magazine" impressed by her first print her mother inspired her to continue writing. Passionate about books started writing again in 2016 only to have her 1st book One Step At a Time come to light in (Dec 2018). Multi- Awardee. Has been invited as Keynote Speaker on various occasions for IIT-Mumbai, Currently the Global Goodwill Ambassador for India.

Foreword

Call it what you will — grit, determination, a can-do attitude — but it all comes down to the same thing: being able to keep going in the face of challenge and even failure is a major component of a person's future and success.

The ability to persist in the face of difficulty may be as essential to success as talent or intelligence.

If you'd like to help yourself develop that confidence and resilience, you may be wondering where to start.

Fortunately, there are a number of proven ways that can foster perseverance and determination in yourself, and in this book, I've shared some of the top tips to raise yourself as a resilient being. At the end of the book, you will feel confident and also be ready to take on the challenges of life, which will in turn help you foster the resilience you need to succeed. And make you come out stronger.

CHAPTER I

The Main Factor: Confidence

If you want to reach the peak of success in life, you have to have self confidence. In fact, I would argue that understanding the importance of self confidence and learning how to acquire it is one of the most important lessons you could ever undertake in life.

Why is Self Confidence Important?

Self confidence is important for many reasons. First and foremost, when you're self confident, it means you believe in yourself. You have full faith in your abilities and in your decision making skills.

Even if you don't know how to do something or achieve something, self confidence gives you the boost you need to find out the answers.

Other people also notice self confidence. Those who are self confident are typically leaders in their families, their communities, and in their workplaces. People are drawn to them and more likely to listen to them and respect them.

What is Self Confidence?

Simply put, self confidence is having trust in your own abilities.

It's a lot different from being overly confident or having an ego. Being falsely confident can cause a lot of problems. Having an ego can cause a lot of problems.

But, when you have genuine self confidence and you believe in yourself, no task or goal seems insurmountable. Even if you come up against something you don't know how to do, you have enough faith in yourself to learn how. Similarly, even if you encounter a difficult decision, self confidence means you trust your ability to choose the best path for you.

What are the Benefits of Self-Confidence?

Having real, true self confidence is important because it's extremely difficult to go through life when you don't trust your own decisions or believe in yourself. When you lack self confidence, you end up looking to others to make decisions for you instead of looking within. This can be dangerous because it means that other people will influence your decisions, rather than you being the primary decision maker in your life.

Of course, it's nice to have mentors and people you look up to who can help you choose a path or help you on your journey. However, the ultimate, final decision need to come from you not them. The benefit of being self confident is that you have peace with your decisions, even if everyone around you doesn't agree with them.

If you're not self confident, it can be easy to be swayed by people who appear to know what they're doing. You might make a choice based on what someone else thinks is right, not what is actually right for your particular situation.

Why is Confidence Important for Success?

Self confidence is clearly evident. The importance of self confidence is that it subconsciously alerts others that they're in the presence of someone who is a leader and sure of themselves. People look up to those who have confidence. People with a strong sense of self and who project their inner confidence are more likely to get raises, promotions, and become successful in life.

How Do You Gain Confidence?

The great news is that no one is born confident. There's no such thing as a confident baby. We all have the ability to become confident people and develop sincere self confidence no matter how we grew up, where we went to school, where we live, or where we work. To put it another way, confidence is an equal playing field, something that's available to everyone.

That said, the primary way to gain self confidence is trying and failing.

Trying and Failing Leads to Self Confidence
It might seem counterintuitive but you become more confident the more you try and fail. Just because someone is confident doesn't mean they're perfect. It doesn't mean they never make mistakes. All it means is that they trust in their abilities. And the way you build trust in yourself is to keep trying again and again no matter how many times you fail.

Once again: no one is born confident. It comes from trying and failing and trying again. Confidence comes from years of trials. The importance of self confidence is that those who have it are the ones who have made the most mistakes and don't mind it at all because they know the mistakes led to their proficiency and then eventual success.

You Can't Become Confident By Playing it Safe.
Confidence doesn't come from playing it safe. You have to have grit. Perseverance. Thick skin. When you go through hard things in life and you attempt something numerous times before actually achieving it, you become strong and self confident. You realize that you can succeed at your goals. Some just happen to take longer than others, and confident people are ok with knowing that. They know the success will eventually come. They believe in themselves because the evidence of their past points to the fact that they don't quit – and when you don't quit, eventually success will happen.

So, really, the importance of self confidence is that when you have it, you always have someone on your side: you. You become so strong that you can walk into any room without someone by your side. Traveling alone doesn't bother you at all. You can set strong boundaries and keep them without feeling guilty. Lastly, you can experience true friendship and true love because you're able to stand independently on your own first. Confidence has so many benefits, but of course, the road to get there isn't easy and that's why many people don't walk it.

Is Confidence the Key to Success?

As evidenced, confidence is a strong indicator of success. But, the importance of self confidence is more than it leading to success. Really, the importance is what it does for you, how you view yourself, how you treat yourself, and how you navigate the world.

Improving your self confidence, whether you start with reading self help books, starting to attend therapy, or simply dressing up more for yourself during the day, is a great way to improve your life overall. Not only will being more confident help you in your relationships and in the workplace, but most importantly, it will help you improve your relationship with yourself.

You only have one life to live, so why not live it confidently? Why not live in a world where you trust your own decisions or instincts? Try it sometime. Try and fail and try again. Immerse yourself in personal development. Give yourself grace. Journal. Allow yourself to understand why you are the way you are, and if you're unhappy with your level of self confidence, take the steps today to improve it. Several small steps and micro improvements over time can lead to massive changes in the way you view yourself and the world in the future.

At the end of the day, the importance of self confidence is that it helps you to be more like you. It can be a bit of a long road to get there, but it's worth every step on the journey.

CHAPTER II

Selfcare is the Most Important

We can all help our loved ones and community members get through crisis. But as we take action to support others, it is also vital that we take the time to support and care for ourselves. This page shares tips and resources to help you practice self-care.

The Importance of Self-Care

While you are supporting and helping someone who may be in crisis, it is especially important for you to also take care of yourself. Practicing self-care does not mean you are choosing yourself over your loved one. It means that you are simply being mindful of your own needs, so you are better able to support the people you care about. When you take care of yourself and are not stressed, you are better able to meet the needs of others.

Self-care comes in a variety of forms. It does not require an elaborate plan; self-care can be as simple as taking a deep breath when you notice you are becoming stressed. By maintaining your physical and mental health, you will likely be better equipped to handle the stressors that come along with supporting someone you care about.

Signs of Stress

Take a look at this list, and check in with yourself. It's important and healthy to acknowledge your limits.

Do you feel...

Anxious or full of worry?

Unable to concentrate?

Achy or sick more than usual?

Sad or generally unhappy?

Overwhelmed and constantly worried?

Irritable or short tempered?

Tired often?

Lonely or alone?

Are you having trouble...

Remembering things?

Relaxing?

Getting your work done?

Making good decisions?

Have you...

Used alcohol, cigarettes, or drugs to "feel better"?

Been sleeping too much or too little?

Been eating too much or too little?

Gained or lost weight?

Isolated yourself from friends and family?

Neglected responsibilities?

Lost interest in activities you used to enjoy?

These can all be signs and symptoms of stress. If you think stress-overload might be affecting your life, there is something you can do about it.

Self-Care Strategies for Managing Stress

Self-care, as the word itself suggests, is what we do to take care of ourselves. When we get stressed out, we tend to ignore the very things that might make us feel better, so it is important to find time to take care of yourself.

Remain socially connected. When you are supporting someone else, it can be easy to lose sight of your other social connections. It is important stay in touch with your family and friends who can offer support. Set aside some time each week to spend time with others in your support network.

Maintain a healthy lifestyle. By improving your physical health, you will be better able to maintain your mental health, and therefore may be more effective in supporting someone you care about.

- Exercising regularly is an important part of staying both physically and mentally healthy. Exercise doesn't have to consist of a complicated workout routine at the gym. It can be as simple as taking the stairs instead of the elevator, or walking or biking instead of driving. Daily exercise produces stress-relieving hormones and improves your general health.
- Eating healthy foods is what will give your body fuel to exercise. By eating mostly unprocessed foods, you can lower your risk for chronic illness and stabilize your energy and mood.
- Getting enough sleep is also important in maintaining your physical and mental health. People generally require 7 – 9 hours of sleep to stay healthy. Turning off your phone and TV about 30 minutes before you go to bed can help you sleep better.

Make time for yourself. When caring for someone who may be suicidal, it can be hard to find time to take care of yourself. However, to be a productive caregiver, it is important to have some "me time." Write out a list of activities that bring you joy to refer to when you need some time for yourself. These activities do not have to be elaborate or take a lot of planning. It can be something as simple as taking a walk in a park, listening to music, or writing in your journal. Anything that makes you feel better is worth a little bit of time out of your day.

CHAPTER III

Can-do Attitude

A can-do attitude is, simply put, a belief that one can tackle whatever comes their way – and a willingness to do it. Whether you are on the 'can' or 'can't' side of things, you probably noticed that how you value yourself and your abilities directly reflects onto how much you can actually do in life. We are, indeed, our best friends or worst enemies. Here I'll explain what a can-do attitude is, where it comes from, and give you seven ways to develop it.

What is a can-do attitude?

You probably know at least one person with a can-do attitude. They are those people with a conviction that anything can be done once they've set their mind to it. It's more than mere optimism, though. Such a belief is combined with a motivation to work on accomplishing the goal or completing the task.

A can-do attitude is a mindset. As such, it is usually deeply ingrained into our psyche. Different factors might contribute to us either being can-doers or doubters, from our temperaments, upbringing, to various experiences we have had throughout our life. Although the can't-do attitude can be a strong habit of mind, we can also retrain ourselves into a different habit.

Indeed, we can learn to change our mindset, believe in ourselves, and – do it!

A can-do attitude is responsible for the great deeds and ideas that came to fruition. Heroism, altruism, change, revolution – none of it exists without such a readiness to make it happen. I witnessed many exceptional contributions to the community during my volunteering years. "We can do it" was so contagious that none of us ever even thought those projects might not succeed.

What's more, technological advancement would have probably ended at just stone tools if it wasn't for those endowed with a can-do attitude. But you don't need a can-do attitude just to make the whole world a better or more evolved place. You need it to challenge yourself to be the best version of yourself you can be – in any field. As a mother of a four-year-old, I know it's safe to say that motherhood is absolutely impossible without such a stance. People who seem to sprint through career advancements, too, are guided by the same attitude: "I can do it!"

7 ways to develop a can-do attitude

Everyone's path towards developing a can-do attitude will differ depending on where you start from. Nonetheless, there are some things everyone can implement to reprogram their mindset. Here are seven ways you can start to develop a can-do attitude.

- **Develop a growth mindset**

The concept of a growth vs fixed mindset was put forth by Carol Dweck, a Stanford University psychologist. In its simplest, fixed mindset means believing that we have unchanging traits. Those characteristics are dictating what and how we can do in life. Thinking of yourself as stupid (or intelligent) would be an example of a fixed mindset.

A growth mindset, on the other hand, is about believing in the effects of exercise and learning. So, you would not suppose that your intelligence got you through school and into a fulfilling career. You would credit all the hard work and time invested instead.

"You don't need a can-do attitude just to make the world a better place. You need it to challenge yourself to be the best version of yourself you can be."

Why would believing you were intelligent, talented, or good be wrong? The problem with a fixed mindset is that once the trait fails to deliver the results you were after, you feel lost. "This isn't working! The only explanation is that I'm not clever enough!" See the logic?

People with a growth mindset are more resilient to stress and associated adverse outcomes (from academic and career underperformance to depression or substance use). In other words, they believe that anything can be achieved – if the necessary effort and thought are put into them.

- **Accept and learn from your mistakes**

Whether you like it or not, you will make mistakes. In a way, being alive means erring. However, are you prone to becoming fixated on your errors or beating yourself up? Or, do you tend to cast blame on others for the circumstances? Both habits are probably preventing you from developing a can-do attitude.

Accepting responsibility is the first step towards learning from your life experience. Self-forgiveness is the next one. The research revealed the ability to use past mistakes constructively and learn from them results in better individual and group/organisation performance.

So, the next time you get it wrong, don't throw sticks and stones at yourself. Analyze. What happened? And what could be done better the next time? Take a moment to feel bad about it – and then move on.

- **Be mindful of opportunities and take them when they come along**

One thing that's usually hard for those who do not have a can-do attitude is to notice and take up new opportunities and chances in life. The comfort of the known feels safe. This is perfectly natural.

However, if you aspire to become someone who believes in themselves, goes out, and gets things done – you need to move outside of your comfort zone. It's not necessary to be extreme and go far beyond what you used to feel comfortable about. Baby steps will get you there, too.

Simply make it your task to start noticing growth opportunities. When you do spot them, ask yourself if maybe you could engage with it? What would feel safe enough, but still bring a bit of change in your life? Do this regularly, and you'll start noticing a new perspective opening up.

- **Focus on being congruent**

When we are trying to transform the way we think about ourselves, we need all the support we can get. In this case, you want your thoughts, actions, and emotions to align. What do we mean by that?

Although some proponents of affirmations would tell you that repeating "I can do it!" would be enough to conquer the world, the reality isn't that simple. A failed attempt at affirming ourselves into greatness will likely result in the psychological discomfort reemerging, a study revealed.

We need to work on changing our thoughts, actions, and feelings and make them all congruent. For example, noticing and changing your thought pattern is one step (we'll get back to it next). However, you need to work out your emotional reactions and understand why you feel the way you do. Is it rational and substantiated, or could you feel in some other way?

Finally, the way you act should also support the can-do attitude. The next time you get the opportunity, make yourself respond to it slightly different to what you're used to. Somewhat more as a can-doer, to be precise.

- **Be mindful of your self-talk**

We all have an inside voice telling us different things. For many, the voice is the harshest critic one could imagine. For those with a can-do attitude, on the other hand, "You got this" is the mantra they hear repeatedly in their head.

A systematic review of nearly 70 scientific papers confirmed the power of self-talk. Positive self-talk can improve our performance, help with depression or anxiety symptoms, and increase our confidence. Reframing your thoughts makes your mind work for you instead of against you. What we think tends to happen. This so-called Pygmalion effect often works both ways.

Therefore, the next time you catch yourself thinking "This is too hard", "It's impossible", "I couldn't possibly do it", stop. Then, come up with alternative statements. Don't go for super-hero level right away. In other words, for affirmations to work, they need to be believable for you. Gradually progress towards automatically thinking positive about yourself, your abilities and your outlook. In that way, you will also start believing that you can do it.

- **Unlearn the learned helplessness**

Psychological experiments have revealed a phenomenon called 'learned helplessness'. In short, dogs were put in a problem situation. Every attempt to resolve it and run away from an adverse stimulus would result in more adversity. Afterwards, even when they could escape or terminate the shock, they would not even try. They learned that they were helpless.

Humans learn this, too, although, thankfully, usually in a much less dramatic manner. Seligman proposed that, in the face of traumatic events that we cannot control, we might become passive, depressive, and stop learning. Such a state could generalise and make us freeze when facing any challenge. Therefore, if you want to change your attitude towards life and challenges, it's time for you to start unlearning the learned helplessness. How?

"One thing that's hard for those who do not have a can-do attitude is to notice and take up new opportunities in life. The comfort of the known feels safe."

One thing that's usually hard for those who do not have a can-do attitude is to notice and take up new opportunities and chances in life. The comfort of the known feels safe. With time, you will accumulate too many arguments against helplessness for your mind to oppose them any longer.

• **Change your locus of control**

One thing that is characteristic of individuals with a can-do attitude is that they have an inner locus of control. Locus of control is a psychological term indicating where you position the power over your experiences. Is it internal or external?

In other words, do you feel that a lot of things are outside of your control? Or do you feel in charge of both your reactions and the events that happen in your life? A study revealed that people with an internal locus of control are healthier, more satisfied, and, overall, have higher subjective well-being levels.

If you want to become a person who believes in themselves and has the zest to accomplish whatever they set their mind to, try shifting your locus of control. How to do it? The majority of the above tips will result in a gradual shift of the locus.

Additionally, try and remember that you always have a choice. Brainstorm your options, talk to people, make lists of pros and cons, whatever works. The choice is always yours. Even when the uncontrollable life events come – you choose how you will see and feel them.

Yes, you can!

If you don't possess a can-do attitude just yet, don't be too harsh on yourself. You're far from being alone. Nonetheless, if you wish to change things, believe that it can be done. You can become one of those people who seem to have it going for them. Their secret? Allow me to respond with a quote: "Everything can be taken from a man but one thing: the last of the human freedoms — to choose one's attitude in any given set of circumstances, to choose one's own way." — Viktor E. Frankl, Man's Search for Meaning •

CHAPTER IV

What Resilience looks like?

Resilience is a life skill that has the potential to make you bulletproof in the face of 'slings and arrows of outrageous fortune.'

You are not born with resilience, you earn it; you realize you have traits of a resilient person when you make it through the tough times with your head held high, not giving in to your negative thoughts or surrendering.

Grit and resilience shows us what humans are made of.

Persevering in the face of impossible odds is no small feat, and when we see another person striving against the odds, we are inspired beyond words.

Resilience is a skill that will guard you against mental and psychological breakdown after a traumatic experience, give you space to improvise when nothing seems to be working, force you to find meaning in life when everything seems pointless, and make you an overall badass.

Let's take a look at resilience in detail in the following sections, and later we will highlight the key traits that make a person resilient.

What is Resilient Behavior?

Resilience in its literal sense means to 'bounce back' or rebound from a traumatic, challenging, and adversarial situation.

If you lose a job, go through a breakup, flunk an exam, or suffer from any tragic misfortune, in the end, it is your ability to accept, adapt, and choose to bounce back that matters for your progress and improvement.

Choosing a logical response to any unfortunate situation by stepping back and taking a breather is the defining trait of a resilient person.

The ability of distancing yourself from tragedy and come up with best coping strategies is why resilient people are so good at bouncing back.

Through sheer resilience, he was not only able to develop a communication system between the prisoners that shared words of inspiration, but also managed to survive the atrocities of the camp all through mental toughness and resilience.

Resilience is closely related to grit and toughness. Truly resilient people never blame outside events for their misfortune.

They are always into improving themselves, eliminating weaknesses and flaws, and developing skills and strategies to make the best of a certain situation.

Humans are by nature story tellers and love to hear a good story.

Stories of resilience inspire us beyond measure. Successful people, like Elon Musk, face setbacks on almost a day to day basis.

Even their childhood has stories of inspiration that how against all odds they chose to rise above their circumstances and changed the world.

Contrary to popular belief, resilience is not a product of wishful optimism detached from reality.

Such misplaced optimism can shatter at any time leading to depression and 'woe-is-me' mentality.

Resilience is not the product of sheer optimism, but a blend of optimism and a reality dose of acceptance.

What Causes a Person to be Resilient?

It is hard to pinpoint the causes of what makes a person

resilient. Resilience, like any other skill, can be learnt, however, there are certain individual traits and environmental factors that influence resilience.

If a person has been through a few wretched experiences in life and somehow managed to pull through, they are more resilient if faced with any future calamity.

Maurice Vanderpol, a pioneering resilience researcher, identified a certain set of skills to tackle with psychological trauma called "plastic shield".

These skills included ability to make associations and to distance oneself from a tragedy along with humor, as the set of "plastic shield" skills that enabled the survivors to persevere through the grueling concentration camp.

Why is it Important to be Resilient?
Resilience makes people adapt with adversity or persevere through hardships without losing their mental health.

Life can put you down one too many times, but if you have resilience you will find ways to overcome adversity.

Resilient people look at problems as temporary bumps in the road. Resilience makes them overcome challenges with whatever they have at their disposal.

Self-confidence comes easily to people who are resilient. They are confident in their abilities to overcome adversity.

If you have ever overcome a few challenges in your life, you will find that you are able to face down minor setbacks with the confidence of an experienced pro.

How to Become More Resilient?
Adaptability is the cornerstone of resilience.

Life is all about change, and if you accept that fact wholeheartedly then you would be ten steps ahead of most people in being more resilient.

Adaptability is an unmistakable sign of resilience in a person.

Adaptability has within it two important aspects of resilience: (1) acceptance; and (2) improvisation.

1. Acceptance

Acceptance is the prerequisite for calling forth the forces of resilience. Keeping yourself in denial about your life situation and avoiding responsibility is the worst way to deal with problems.

Resilience is not about avoidance but confronting problems head on. It is the fighter's mentality that counts when it comes to resilience.

2. Improvisation

Improvisation is your ability to make do with whatever life throws at you. As the saying goes, "when life throws you lemons, make lemonade".

We can't always guarantee that everything that we plan will go accordingly.

Most often than not, plans go sideways, projects derail, relationships get stormy, and life takes an unexpected turn for the worse.

In such situations, it will be your ability to improvise that will rescue you.

Resilience is an aspect of your mental health, and that's why when you don't take care of yourself by eating well, sleeping for appropriate amount of time, and exercising, your resilience can suffer.

10 Traits of a Resilient Person

So now that we know a little about what makes a resilient person, their characteristics, and about causes and signs of a resilient person, let's look at the 10 traits of a resilient person.

1. Having a Growth Mentality

Growth mentality is looking at problems as opportunities to grow.

It is that change in perspective that can make you infinitely more resilient than the other guy.

2. Self-Awareness

Resilient people are self-aware. Self-awareness about their feelings, their thoughts, and their behaviors lets resilient people come up with better stress-coping strategies.

3. Keeping it Real

A resilient person will never hide behind empty optimism or stay in denial. Resilience means that you are accepting of reality and making sure you take action to remedy it.

4. Perseverance

Not taking 'no' for an answer is another trait that resilient people have. It is important to understand that resilience is as much about persevering and fighting for what you believe as it is about change.

Sometimes, you have to show resolve and not budge from your principles to be resilient.

5. Having an Internal Locus of Control

An internal locus of control means that you don't blame outside circumstances for the position you are in, but you look for areas of growth and weaknesses in yourself that you need to put effort into.

6. Detachment from Self-Centered Emotions

Resilient people are like Zen masters who are detached from their egoistic whims, fantasies, and negative thinking.

Detachment from ego gives resilient people that much mental space to avoid being sucked into the ego's negative thoughts.

By doing so, they avoid a lot of mental drama later on.

7. Healthy Optimism

Optimism that does not border on wishful thinking is good for buttressing resilience.

Optimism is that ray of hope in a sea of darkness that seems to surround one going through tough times.

8. Having Self-Compassion

Engaging in negative self-talk, blaming yourself for your circumstances, and constantly degrading yourself with your inner voice will ultimately lead to spiraling down into depression, stress, and worry.

Resilient people are self-compassionate, and consider themselves to be above the challenges that face them.

9. They Have a Support System

A support system consists of your friends and family. People who are there for you when you going through tough times.

They can offer words of encouragement and motivation to get you back on track.

10. Exploring Options

Exploring your options before making a decision is another trait that differentiates a resilient person. Since they have the psychological space, they can logically assess their situation and consider options.

Resilience is an extremely important life skill. It helps us bounce back after a setback, makes us endure hardship with a positive attitude, and helps us find meaning within tragedies. Resilience is hard to measure and scientifically examine, but we know it once we see someone making an all-out effort against the odds.

CHAPTER V

Know when and how to step in.....

Are you looking in every direction and feeling confused about what to do next in your life? Are you paralyzed with fear from making a move because change feels scary? Or are you feeling stagnant and going through the motions, daydreaming about how your life could be different? If only I could win the lottery, etc....

Perhaps you have been contemplating your purpose to figure out why you are here. You have reached a state of feeling like you just don't know what to do.

Some people know early on what they are destined to do regarding career and family life. They go to school, start working in their chosen field, and live a happy and fulfilled life. Some people make a major change in mid-life (the mid-life crisis!). Other people may change and re-invent themselves multiple times throughout their life.

No one way is better than another. If you have reached a state of not knowing what to do with your life, this is a good thing. It's a sign that things need to change – and that change is just around the corner.

Whether you are facing a decision of what to do next in your personal or professional life, here are five steps you can follow:

5 Steps To Help You Find Out What To Do Next In Life
1. Take Time Out

The first thing you should do, if you don't know what to do, is do nothing. Take time out to sit with the unknown. You don't have to hide away from the world by going away on a retreat for a month to sort out your life. But if you can do this, then more power to you!

Taking time out could mean cutting back on non-essential tasks and activities, freeing up more time each day for you to just 'be.'

Allow yourself to get still, to reconnect to your inner being. Whether you do this by spending time alone in nature, journaling, meditation, or some other way, it's important that you clear the clutter of your mind.

You can get stuck in a state of not knowing because there are too many choices. The mind is running these choices over and over again as possibilities, which can be overwhelming.

Take time out to realign your core values and to examine your current state. Ask yourself what is really important to you in life. This is a process; you don't need to make a decision this minute. So take the pressure off of yourself.

2. Feel Your Emotions
With a little extra time to yourself, you may find that feelings will surface that were previously hidden away or covered up because you were too busy.

You cannot avoid your emotions (although many people try by indulging in addictive behaviors). When you feel and examine your emotions, you will find that they have something to teach you.

You may be experiencing doubt, apathy, or even panic about your future. Emotions left unattended to by the conscious mind, such as anger or frustration, can manifest in your body in a physical form (e.g. upset stomach). Don't ignore them.

What often keeps people in a state of indecision is fear. Fear is at the root of many of the so-called negative emotions. But fear could also be mixed with excitement, hope, and elation.

There is a wide spectrum of emotions to be experienced – feel whatever is arising and know that these will eventually pass. The more time you spend acknowledging what you feel, the less scary your emotions will seem over time.

3. Explore Your Passions

With more free time and an increasing understanding of your emotions, next, you will want to explore what brings you joy.

Ask yourself what you feel passionate about. Maybe nothing comes to mind right away. This can feel defeating. But don't worry: you don't have to go out and save the world with a grandiose plan.

What little things or activities bring you joy? What are your hobbies? Spend more time doing what you love or try something new. It will take your focus away from thinking too much about what to do with your life. When you are joyful, it sets you up to be in a position of receiving more joy – like attracts like.

If you're still stuck for ideas, seek out trusted people for support. Listen to others, but DON'T get caught up in their opinions. At the end of the day, only YOU know what is right for you.

If you're enjoying this article, make sure to check out our collection of words of wisdom to bring out the best in you.

4. Take Inspired Action

Can you recall a time in your life when you tried everything in your power to make something happen but it just wasn't happening? Chances are that this path wasn't meant for you, or the timing wasn't right. The universe had other plans for you.

As you explore your passions, it's vital for you to take inspired action. Inspired action means you really feel good about taking the next step and you are moving ahead with conscious awareness. If you are just doing things because you feel you have to, you might be addicted to being busy and not even know it, and ultimately left feeling overwhelmed.

If you're trying too hard to figure out your life, or taking on too many new things to find out your passions, then it's time to go back to step one and take a break!

We are conditioned to believe that nothing can be achieved without hard work. It's true that nothing will happen without taking any action.

However, it's the intention behind your action that can make things easy or difficult for you. Line up your energy first and approach your next step from an inspired state. Life will unfold as it's meant to.

5. Let Go Of The Outcome

You may refuse to take a step forward in life because you don't know what to expect. You don't know the outcome; therefore, fear creeps in. This keeps you in a state of inaction. But what if you let go of the outcome?

How boring would life be if you knew from day one exactly how each day would turn out? There is a sense of intrigue when you don't know precisely how life will be when faced with changing direction.

Don't let fear stop you from exploring possibilities. Remain open to whatever life presents. You may be surprised with an even better outcome than you could have imagined.

It's OK not to know what to do in life at times. Change can be scary – if you tell yourself that it is. However, change is inevitable and it brings growth.

You can't bury your head in the sand forever and ignore what change is trying to teach you. Well, you can bury your head in the sand for a while. But life has a wonderful way of encouraging (sometimes forcing) you to change when you stop going with the flow.

Embrace the unknown for a while. Follow these five steps to prevent yourself from being stuck in indecision for months or years.

CHAPTER VI

Challenge yourself even in times of struggle

When was the last time you challenged yourself and did something outside of your comfort zone? For me, it used to not happen very often. I've always struggled with change and had a pretty small comfort zone.

Over the past few years, I've grown a lot as a person. I've challenged myself to try new experiences and meet new people, putting myself in situations that previously I probably would have avoided.

It turns out, challenging yourself can lead to a lot of personal growth! Here, I'm sharing 22 ways to challenge yourself to live your best life, as well as sharing WHY you should challenge yourself.

Why You Should Challenge Yourself

It can be tempting to live our lives just staying in our comfort zone. I was like that for years! But I also now know the value of challenging yourself and getting outside of your comfort zone.

There are so many reasons to why it's important to challenge yourself. First of all, you'll discover that you are capable of things you didn't think you were. This is a big one I found out about myself. You have so many skills that you could have if you just gave yourself the chance.

By challenging yourself, you'll also reach new goals you never would have previously thought to even reach for. Things that never would have seemed possible for you could be within your grasp.

Sure, you could just stay in your comfort zone and never grow beyond that. No one can force you out of it. But I promise you'll be happy you took the leap!

How to Challenge Yourself

SET A NEW GOAL

I can't think of any better way to challenge yourself than to set a new goal for yourself and really create a plan to follow through on it. There is so much power in goal setting!

If you find yourself hoping to see something change in your life, set a big goal for yourself. But don't stop there! Once you've set your goal, break it down into actionable steps and put them on your calendar.

LEARN A NEW LANGUAGE

Learning a new language is such a fun way to challenge yourself by expanding your horizons. Even better if you love to travel, and can learn the language of some of the places you're going to be visiting!

When it comes to learning a new language, the Duolingo app is my favorite place to start for at least learning the basics.

TAKE A CLASS ABOUT SOMETHING THAT INTERESTS YOU

I am a lifelong learner and I really love and look forward to being able to learn new things. But not everyone is like that. For some people, learning something new is outside their comfort zone.

Taking a class to learn something new is such an amazing experience though! First of all, you might end up like me, creating a business that never would have occurred to you before.

You also might end up making a new friend or finding a new favorite hobby!

WAKE UP EARLIER IN THE MORNING

Mornings can be an amazing time of day. It's a peaceful time to do something like meditate, do yoga, or just sip a cup of coffee before the chaos of the day sets in.

It's also amazing how freaking productive your day can be if you start off on the right foot in the morning.

I know mornings used to be terrible for me. I would turn off so many alarms and stumble into work a little late and a lot stressed. Finally committing to waking up earlier and doing a morning routine made such a big difference in my productivity and mood for the day!

SET A BEDTIME FOR YOURSELF

Going along with the idea of waking up earlier in the morning, I really challenge you to set a bedtime for yourself!

I always tell myself that I need to start going to bed earlier. But the only time I actually do is when I set a bedtime for myself and commit to it.

REACH OUT TO SOMEONE YOU LOOK UP TO

Since starting a business, I have come across so many people I look up to. People I would love to connect with or have a conversation with.

But I never did anything about it.

But once I started reaching out to people I looked up to, I was so glad I did! Sometimes it was to ask for advice, other times it was just to say hi and let them know I enjoyed what they were putting out into the world.

Find something who is kicking ass at what you want to kick ass at and just shoot them an email and tell them how much you admire them! If a relationship doesn't form, at least you'll be able to give them a self-esteem boost.

UNPLUG FROM TECHNOLOGY FOR A DAY

We are so reliant on technology these days, it's almost a

little scary. I mean, have you ever found yourself opening your phone, only to forget why you picked it up in the first place?

So many times a day we check our phones just out of habit!

Not only is it often just a waste of time, but we're shutting ourselves off from connections with the people around us.

I challenge you to turn off the smartphone and close down the computer and TV for an entire day. Instead, just focus on interacting with people and enjoying activities you don't normally make time for like reading a book, having a deep conversation, or spending time in nature.

SET A SAVINGS GOAL

Setting a savings goal can definitely be a challenge, and an especially uncomfortable one if it means cutting your spending to reach your goal. But in the long run, you'll be so glad you challenged yourself in this way.

When I have a trip or another large expense I'm planning for, I always like to break it down and determine how much I need to be saving every month in order to reach my goal. Sometimes I can fit that within my current spending, but often times it means cutting spending in other areas.

WRITE IN A JOURNAL EVERY DAY

As a kid, I kept a journal pretty regularly. As an adult, however, I struggled to stay consistent for a long time.

And yet I've found that when I consistently journal, or at least journal when I'm having a lot of thoughts running around in my head, that it helps keep my anxiety at bay.

If you're someone who has a lot of anxious thoughts, I challenge you to start writing in a journal every day, at least until you have time to figure out if it's helpful for you.

RECONNECT WITH AN OLD FRIEND

We all have those old friends who we still consider friends, but who we probably don't reach out to all that often. Sometimes, it can be easier to just let things be than it is to put in the effort to revive the friendship.

As someone who has had a chance to reconnect with old friends, I can say it's been an amazing experience for me! Those people were in your life for a reason, so it's worth working for those friendships!

START A NEW WORKOUT ROUTINE

Sticking to a workout routine can be so tough! We have the best of intentions, but then we talk ourselves out of it after we've had a long day. Or we just forget about it altogether!

The best way I've found to stick to my workouts is to prepare everything ahead of time and make my intention know. For example, if I wanted to do yoga in the morning before work, I would tell my boyfriend my plan, and then I would get my yoga mat set up the night before so it's there waiting for me in the morning.

I also love using habit trackers to motivate me to stick to a new habit!

TRAVEL TO A NEW PLACE

I know a lot of people who take annual vacations or weekend getaways but always visit the same location. It's great if you've found a place you love so much you want to keep going back, but I also think it can be amazing to travel to new places. And you never know, you might find your new favorite!

Some of my favorite experiences have been being able to travel to new cities, states, or countries, and I'm definitely looking forward to exploring more new places in the future!

TALK TO A STRANGER

I'm not a super outgoing person, and more often than not

I'm the one to pull out my phone to avoid talking to the stranger sitting next to me or riding in the elevator with me. It's not great, but hey, I'm working on it.

When I remember, I occasionally challenge myself to talk to one new person. I especially try to do this if I'm attending an event alone that I'm not super comfortable going to. Jumping into a conversation with someone always helps ease the discomfort!

DITCH ONE BAD HABIT

Let's be honest, we all have at least one or two bad habits we'd like to ditch.

I know how difficult it can be to kick a bad habit.

My favorite source for learning about all-things habits is James Clear and his book Atomic Habits. In the book, he outlines a roadmap to eliminating bad habits, and creating good habits!

For someone who always struggled to declutter previously, I thought this would be so much more difficult for me, but it was actually a breath of fresh air.

If you're struggling to figure out where to start, I always like to start with my clothes! And if you really want to go all in, pick up a copy of The Life-Changing Magic of Tidying Up and get to work!

TRY COOKING A NEW RECIPE

In the interest of full disclosure, I am not a good cook. I'm not terrible, I just don't really know what I'm doing in the kitchen. Plus I'm spoiled because my boyfriend loves to cook, so he does all of our cooking.

That being said, every once in a while I get the urge to whip up a new recipe for myself. It doesn't always go great, but it's fun and helps me work on my cooking skills a bit.

Bonus points if you actually can cook well and use this challenge to grow your cooking abilities to an even more expert level!

VOLUNTEER FOR A CAUSE YOU CARE ABOUT

We all have causes that are near and dear to us, but I'm guessing most of us don't actually make the time to donate our time to those causes. Sure, a monthly donation is great. But so is showing up to help at a local nonprofit!

Volunteering is not only a great way to contribute to your community, but it is also a great way to meet new people and possibly make some new friends.

LEARN TO MEDITATE

For years I saw people I followed online raving about meditation. It wasn't just self improvement bloggers either. All of the most successful online business owners I followed talked about their meditation habit.

Then I read Tribe of Mentors by Tim Ferriss, where he interviews some of the most high-performing people in the world. And in interview after interview, the subject talked about the importance of meditation.

My meditation game is still a little rough, but it's been a fun challenge, and I really have noticed a difference during the weeks I meditate regularly.

MAKE A NEW FRIEND

I remember one of the biggest changes when I graduated from college and moved out of my college town was that I suddenly didn't have all of my friends around. Since I'm not all that outgoing, it's more of a challenge for me to make new friends, and it really forces me to put myself out there.

It's so worth it though! Every time I have put myself out there and made a new friend, I've been so grateful that I did. It can be a lot of fun to make new friends who have similar hobbies or interests.

ASK FOR HELP

Asking for help is scary for a lot of people. Maybe you're

like me and you're a perfectionist, afraid of admitting to someone that you can't do something just right. Or maybe you're afraid of looking stupid. Or afraid of putting yourself out there and talking to someone new. Or afraid of bothering someone with your problem.

There are so many reasons you might avoid asking for help, but most of us do find a reason. I challenge you to ask for help next time you are struggling with something!

START A GRATITUDE JOURNAL

Starting a gratitude journal was a challenge for me! First of all, I thought it was kind of a dumb idea. I really didn't think it would have any effect on my outlook on life.

But even more than that, sometimes you're just in a mood where you want to be negative. You want to focus on the things that are going wrong. And challenging that by forcing yourself to look at the GOOD is uncomfortable.

But writing down things I'm grateful for has actually had such an amazing impact, and it can turn my bad mood right around.

CREATE A VISION BOARD

At first glance, creating a vision board doesn't seem like something that you challenge you. But you'll figure out that it really is!

That's because creating a vision board requires you to do a couple of uncomfortable things. First of all, it forces you to actually create a vision for your future. If you've just been letting life lead you rather than leading your life, it might be scary to create a vision for what you want your life to look like.

Second, creating a vision board forces you to confront your big goals each and every day. So many of us have a big pie in the sky goal that we'll probably never really create a plan to reach. But by creating a vision board, you're constantly reminding yourself of that goal and daring yourself to take action on it.

It's honestly a way of tricking yourself into going after your big scary goals!

There are so many fun ways you can challenge yourself to grow as a person. And the great thing about this list is everyone can find at least one thing on it that sounds like something they can do! And bonus points for doing a bunch of them!

As someone who has always been reserved and had a small comfort zone, I've tried to challenge myself more as an adult to expand my horizons and come out of my shell a bit.

It's made such a huge difference for me, and I know it can do the same for you!

CHAPTER VII

Power of Passion

There is much heart and soul that goes into being successful in business. You need to ask yourself if these elements exist within you regarding the business you are choosing. Are the tasks involved in this business the kind of thing that you will find joy in completing? Will you be working with the type of people who inspire you? Is it a product that you believe in? Passion is essential to your success. When you do what you love to do, you can go beyond success; you can make a real difference in people's lives. With your passion, you can inspire others to find their dreams too.

When you find your passion it will be like a mission. It is something that you know that you were meant to do. When you are following passion, the ups and downs of a business will not get in your way as your passion is stronger than the challenges of your business success or failure. This is one of the reasons you should follow your passion. It will guide you through the rough waters.

Successful people know that passion is energy. It is what drives people to succeed. Without passion towards what you are doing, you do not have a why. When you do not have a why, the how is hard to find.

This energy is contagious. If you spend time with passionate people, it is bound to rub off on you. So if you have not yet found your passion, find people who have. You will soon see a change in your success. As you spend time with passionate, successful people, success skills will start to manifest in your live too. Successful people understand that in order to achieve, they must love what they do. So find something that you love to do and you will be following your passion. Passion is the fastest way to massive success.

Bringing passion to the workplace will assist you in making better decisions, you get more things done in less time. You will want to contribute so much more, that will in turn bring you back more. People will see your passion and they will believe in you and your products and services. You will be trusted and supported by your customers and associates.

Once you have found your passion, you will want to cultivate it. When you start to turn up the heat on your passion, you are bringing more joy and with this you will accomplish success in business and more of your goals.

Your passion can be fueled by helping others to achieve the success that they desire as well. It has been said by the famous speaker, Zig Ziegler, If you help enough people get what they want, you will get EVERYTHING you want. Your passion towards your business will also assist you in creating a great reputation, which will become invaluable in building a more successful operation.

Identify your passion and when you do take the steps to bring it into your life. With passion you can be the best at what you do, and through that you can achieve financial freedom. Once you become abundant, you will be able to assist the world in ways that will fulfill your purpose in life and bring to you all of the joy that life has, rich in successful achievement for all you do.

CHAPTER VIII

How Perseverance works wonders

WHAT IS PERSEVERANCE?
At its simplest, perseverance is the act of working toward your goal despite challenges and setbacks. It's the persistence you display, even if there is a delay in achieving goals or success. People who have long-term goals often lose focus and direction. It's difficult not to lose motivation and enthusiasm after a certain point; however, perseverance teaches you how to continue working hard until you succeed.

Perseverance boils down to the drive and resilience you display while completing an objective. Irrespective of the challenges that emerge or the time it takes you to complete the task, you persist tirelessly and pursue your set goal(s). It's an important quality in life as it allows you to stay in the game even though everything else says it's time to call it quits. Perseverance helps you achieve your life's dreams, goals and vision.

WHY IS PERSEVERANCE IMPORTANT?
Perseverance in the face of challenges indicates leadership qualities. As already highlighted in the above examples of perseverance, individuals who demonstrate perseverance are more likely to succeed in life, especially professional life. Perseverance is a sign of stepping outside your comfort zone and staying focused on your efforts. It also means that you have a growth mindset, that is, the belief that you can develop essential qualities through your efforts. This is a highly valuable quality that organizations actively seek when they're hiring.

HERE'S WHY YOU NEED TO PRIORITIZE PERSEVERANCE AND TAKE STEPS TOWARD DEVELOPING THIS QUALITY IN YOUR LIFE:

- **LEADS TO MASTERY**

You may not know how to do something, even though you're passionate about it. It's perseverance that'll help you attempt and pursue something, in addition to doing your best. Rome wasn't built in a day; you need to be patient because hard work will eventually pay off. Sustained efforts over time can even lead you to master a new skill. You can excel as long as you stay determined.

- **MAKES YOU RESILIENT**

Say you were rejected after five job interviews. You can either quit looking for a job or refuse to give up. Perseverant people don't quit easily. They will continue to rise up to challenges and continue to work hard. Therefore, you become resilient as you power through difficulties and continue to step outside your comfort zone. You continue to grow emotionally as well.

- **TEACHES HOW TO MANAGE CRISES**

Perseverance teaches you how to focus on solutions instead of problems. For example, if something goes wrong, perseverant individuals will identify ways to mitigate a crisis. They know how to stay calm and carry on. In other words, they look at the bigger picture and not abandon a situation or responsibility midway.

The importance of perseverance lies in the fact that it makes you optimistic about the future. You learn not to give up because you believe that the power remains in your hand, as long as you keep at it.

THE IMPORTANCE OF PERSEVERANCE IN CURRENT TIMES

With the rise of small businesses and start-up enterprises, the scope of entrepreneurship continues to expand. However, only a few businesses take flight and succeed in establishing themselves. There are several qualities required in starting and running your own business. Some of them include ambition, intelligence and creativity but most of all, you need perseverance. Without it, sometimes, even the best among us gets it wrong.

Perseverance skills can teach you how to bounce back from disappointment or failure. If you're a professional, consider these qualities of perseverant leaders to effectively navigate business environments and career advancement:

THEY KEEP ASKING WHY

People who persevere are the ones who continue to ask 'why'. It serves as a constant motivator and keeps you on track. It can be as simple as: why am I doing this? The more you remind yourself, the clearer your purpose gets. This is what keeps pushing you.

THEY HAVE SELF-BELIEF

You may have heard people say: if you don't believe in yourself, how will they? If you want to achieve anything, you need to believe in your skills and qualities. Every successful leader believes in themselves and believes in the change they want to make in the world. Fostering your self-belief can help you persevere better.

THEY MAKE ROOM FOR VULNERABILITY

It isn't easy to face your failures and it especially isn't easy to ask for help. Successful people persevere because they know how to learn from their mistakes and overcome setbacks. Instead of giving up easily, they know how to pick themselves up and ask for help. They aren't afraid of being vulnerable and connect with others in times of need. It's okay to share your struggles with people you can trust.

It's important to remember that perseverance is the direct result of our habits. The more we overcome our fears and challenges, the more resilient we become.

HOW TO DEVELOP PERSEVERANCE

As we've already established, perseverance skills are critical to workplace success. Moreover, these skills can be developed over time through patience and practice. Let's look at several ways in which you can improve your perseverance skills:

REJECT THE URGE TO QUIT

The first step to build a perseverance mindset is to reject the urge to give up or quit. If you're unable to accomplish something, give yourself time. Start again the next day. Remind yourself of the reason you're doing it and the ultimate objective you want to achieve.

CREATE AN ACTION PLAN

A detailed action plan can help you remain focused on every objective. It should account for your journey from start to completion. The primary benefit of the plan is that it holds you accountable and helps you keep track of your progress. The more you monitor, the easier it is to stay motivated.

PRIORITIZE IMPROVEMENT

At the core of perseverance lies the act of getting out of your comfort zone. You need to make peace with the fact that you need to work on self-improvement. Establishing higher standards of excellence for yourself is a good place to start. As you continue to strengthen perseverance, you continue to grow as a well-rounded individual.

While these strategies are useful in keeping you focused on your goals, it's equally important to accommodate things that you care for. When you're passionate about something and enjoy doing those tasks, it's easier to stay on track; otherwise, it may start to feel like a burden.

PRACTICE EXCELLENCE, STRENGTHEN PERSEVERANCE

Perseverance is a skill that employers highly value because they need people who can power through tough circumstances.

CHAPTER IX

Grit the main ingredient

The word "grit" was coined by Angela Lee Duckworth, a psychologist, and researcher. She defined the term as "passion and perseverance for long-term and meaningful goals." Grit is your ability to continue with your passion relentlessly, even in the face of obstacles. In the 21st century, grit is the new hype when it comes to personal success.

The passion of grit is not infatuation or strong emotions, but commitment and a clarity of direction. Such passion is vital for staying committed to a task, no matter how boring or difficult it may be. Let's learn more about why grit is an outstanding quality and how it can help you develop your mind.

Why is grit important?

Many of us are conditioned to believe that it takes talent and intelligence to succeed. But grit is what brings you the extra mile towards success - think of it as the flavor packet in your instant noodles. Sure, being smart and talented is a big deal, but you cannot truly thrive without grit. Your ability to persevere in the face of adversity is what drives your success and achievements.

According to Duckworth, the ability to be gritty—to pursue what's important to you and be resilient in the face of failure—is a crucial component of success independent of and beyond what talent and intelligence contribute.

All the talent in an individual could just as easily remain as unmet potential, without the presence of grit. For talent to transform into a skill that leads you to success, grit is what you need.

How grit can develop your mind

Grit can imply different things to different people: some see it as mental toughness or mental strength. When it comes to using grit to develop and transform your mind, you need to define first what grit means to you. It could be going to the gym every day for a month, or learning to play the violin or catching up with one friend every weekend. Define an area in your life where you feel you could use more grit.

Once you have a clear purpose in mind, use the following tools to develop grit and improve your mind.

Practice

Grit has a lot to do with perseverance. For developing your perseverance, it helps to practice deliberately and regularly. Even if you fail, take feedback on what can be improved from every attempt. Dedicated practice will help make grit a habit that not only makes you more skilled at what you do but will also help develop the courage to keep going when things get tough.

Purpose

Your purpose is something you can be interested in for the long haul. Without purpose, practice is meaningless. A keen interest in what you do, and being able to hold that interest long-term is essential. Rather than longing for a natural calling to hit you like an epiphany, find something that encourages you to keep learning the more you practice it.

Hope

The world revolves on hope, and that's what you need to remember when developing grit for mental strength. It is the quality that you need most when facing inevitable setbacks. Failure is a necessary part of life, but if you see it as an opportunity to learn, improve, and get back on your feet, it will only increase your likelihood of succeeding in future endeavors. Stay hopeful and positive, and know that it's okay to fail as long as you keep going.

Time

The last, but not the least, in our grit formula is the element of time. Success is not an overnight story. It takes long years of dedicated practice, with a clear purpose in mind, and staying relentlessly hopeful in the face of failure to achieve your goals. Instead of getting frustrated, be patient, and give yourself the time needed to keep learning and stay in the game.

Rather than impressive amounts of courage or inspiration, grit is a far more grounded quality. Build daily habits that help you stick to a schedule. This will allow you to conquer both challenges and distractions consistently. Your mental strength shows through in your consistency, more than in courage, talent, or intelligence. Achieving your goals is as simple as showing up to put in the effort every single day. And that's why you need grit.

CHAPTER X

Psychology of Success

"Success is not final; failure is not fatal: It is the courage to continue that counts." — Winston S. Churchill

"It is better to fail in originality than to succeed in imitation." — Herman Melville

"The road to success and the road to failure are almost exactly the same." — Colin R. Davis

Notice anything these have in common?

All three involve success and failure. There's a reason for this, and it's the key behind the psychology of success and failure.

The Deal with Failure

It turns out that failure is one of humanity's greatest strengths, and therefore is not the opposite of success, but actually a key factor in meeting our goals. This has been proven by evolutionary scientists such as Charles Darwin, who is credited with saying, "it is not the strongest of the species that survives. It is the one that is most adaptable to change."

Changing and adapting is just what humans have done over centuries of evolution. For example, we realized early on that we're too weak to hunt as individuals — our bodies are too fragile — so we adapted by hunting in groups, which evolved into ever more complex communities, using our collective abilities that have led to not only our ability to survive, but also thrive.

Babies learn through this same mechanism. We're born helpless, but gradually learn how to point at what we want so caregivers understand what we need. Through further trial and error — by making mistakes and failing sometimes — this eventually helps us learn to walk, talk, and grow into a fully realized adult human.

In short, though it seems counterintuitive, we are designed to turn weakness into our greatest source of strength. It's through our failures that we learn how we need to adapt and grow in order to be successful, whether that success is finding our next meal or launching a complex business venture.

Key Factors Behind Success

The good news is that the key traits needed for success — growth mindset, grit, and psychological flexibility — can be cultivated.

Growth Mindset

How we view and manage failure helps cultivate success in our lives, and that starts with having a growth mindset. A growth mindset means that we believe through hard work and effort we can grow and learn, even in the face of failure. It means we believe mastery is possible if we keep trying, keep taking chances, and work toward improving. Failure is not a permanent condition.

"When we believe that abilities are fixed (fixed mindset), we interpret failure as evidence for the lack of ability, and we stop trying," writes Louai Rahal, based on psychologist Carol Dweck's work. "When we believe that abilities can be stretched with learning (growth mindset), we perceive failures as opportunities for learning and we reflect on failures in order to stretch our abilities."

Grit

In order to stretch our abilities, we next need grit, "a combination of passion and perseverance," says Lee. Having grit means relentlessly pursuing goals and not allowing setbacks to deter progress. It's more than talent, more than smarts, it's a practice of constantly learning and putting in the effort.

"Grit is having stamina," said professor and TED speaker Angela Duckworth. "Grit is sticking with your future day in, day out, not just for the week, not just for the month, but for years, and working really hard to make that future a reality. Grit is living life like it's a marathon — not a sprint."

Psychological Flexibility

To move forward with a growth mindset and grit, the final ingredient is psychological flexibility, or the ability to adapt behavior to a constantly changing world and the changing needs we find ourselves facing.

"Having psychological flexibility lets people think outside of the box and be creative when confronted with an obstacle," says Lee. "It also allows a person to change course as needed if what [they have] been doing hasn't been working."

With these key traits we can learn to harness failure as a tool to move forward and persevere to be successful, but we probably can't be successful by trying to do this alone.

Don't Go Through it Alone

Just like humans' adaptive ability to work together as a community while hunting to avoid danger, it's important for our success to reach out for help when we need it. Humans aren't built to be solitary, lone creatures. We need connection and support from other people, on our worst days and even when we're striving for our best.

"People who are successful also learn to accept help from others; they don't try to do everything by themselves," says Lee. "They have insight into their own limitations and are comfortable going to others with strengths in their areas of growth."

At the end of the day, there's no reason to be afraid of failure. In fact, it's a critical piece for success itself, the very reason we keep growing, learning, thriving, and ultimately, succeeding.

CHAPTER XI

Fostering your mindset for growth

Mindset stems from our own set of powerful beliefs. A growth mentality assumes that views can be changed when they no longer allow us to achieve our goals. Here are five ways you can take control of your mental attitude to foster a growth mindset:

1. Embrace failure

Fostering a growth mentality involves viewing failure as a positive rather than a negative. Everyone has setbacks. The key is to learn from each one and improve your decision making. Wildly successful people typically fail their way to success. Steven Spielberg was rejected from film school three times before getting his big break. Even Oprah Winfrey was fired from her news coanchor position at a Baltimore TV station before going on to build a successful daytime talk show. A producer reportedly told her that she was "unfit for television news." Oprah later said, "I had no idea what I was in for or that this was going to be the greatest growing period of my adult life."

2. Become a lifelong learner

People with a growth mindset actively seek learning opportunities which result in more career success. Be curious about everything. Research shows that, while less successful people read mostly for entertainment, those at the top are avid readers of self-improvement books. In fact, 85% of successful people read two or more self-improvement or educational books per month. Another study revealed that 30% of executives said having a willingness to keep learning is the characteristic they consider most necessary for an employee to succeed.

3. Seek out challenge

Challenges are opportunities that propel you forward towards your goals and help you grow. According to C.S. Lewis, "Hardships often prepare ordinary people for an extraordinary destiny." Don't underestimate the power of being able to overcome obstacles. Are you feeling too comfortable in your current career? That may be an indication that it's time to seek out new challenges. After all, the magic happens outside your comfort zone.

4. Go beyond your limits

Another way to foster a growth mentality is to push yourself beyond what you think you can do. In one interesting study, researchers asked participants to cycle as hard as they could for 4,000 meters. Later, participants were given the same instructions but were able to race against an avatar of their previous ride. What they didn't know was that the avatar was going faster than they did previously. The result was that participants rode alongside their avatar, going significantly further than they did the first time. When you push yourself, you can surpass even your own expectations.

5. Ask for feedback

People who want to grow personally and professionally tend to ask for and value feedback. This is because growth-oriented individuals are interested in developing and challenging themselves. They aren't afraid to be criticized or judged. Once you understand that you are responsible for your own growth, you will have the confidence to ask for feedback and learn from it.

A CHANGING WORLD

With technology and business models changing rapidly, embracing a growth mindset is vital to career success.

Workers will need to continuously learn new skills to remain competitive as automation technologies, including artificial intelligence, become more prevalent. According to a report by McKinsey, up to 375 million workers worldwide will need to change roles or learn new skills by 2030. Research shows that your mindset predicts achievement. It's not how good you are but how good you want to be that matters.

www.ingramcontent.com/pod-product-compliance
Lightning Source LLC
Chambersburg PA
CBHW050132170726

47995CB00001BA/447